World's Scariest Places

Isolated Islands

Alix Wood

Gareth Stevens Publishing

Please visit our website, **www.garethstevens.com**. For a free color catalog of all our high-quality books, call toll free 1-800-542-2595 or fax 1-877-542-2596.

Cataloging-in-Publication Data

Names: Wood, Alix.
Title: Isolated islands / Alix Wood.
Description: New York : Gareth Stevens Publishing, 2020. | Series: World's scariest places | Includes glossary and index.
Identifiers: ISBN 9781538242599 (pbk.) | ISBN 9781538242025 (library bound) | ISBN 9781538242605 (6 pack)
Subjects: LCSH: Islands--History--Anecdotes--Juvenile literature. | Haunted places--Juvenile literature. | Ghosts--Juvenile literature.
Classification: LCC BF1461.W64 2020 | DDC 133.10914'2--dc23

First Edition

Published in 2020 by
Gareth Stevens Publishing
111 East 14th Street, Suite 349
New York, NY 10003

Produced for Gareth Stevens by Alix Wood Books
Designed by Alix Wood
Editor: Eloise Macgregor

Photo credits:
Cover, 1, 4 inset, 6, 7 bottom, 10-11, 14, 15, 22, 23, 27, 28 © Adobe Stock Images; 4-5 © LPLT; 5 inset © J. Wood Laing; 7 top © Naturenet; 8-9 © Kevin53; 9 inset © Flikr/Wa17gs; 10 inset © Uwe Küchler; 12, 13 © Wayne Batzer; 16 © Biswarup Ganguly; 17 © Amol Hatwar; 20 © Denis Bin; 21 inset © Harvey Bond; 25 top inset © Fumihiko Ueno; 26 Bottom inset © Harold T. Ng; 26-27 © Chris Combe; 29 top © Brent Hellickson; all other images are Creative Commons

Printed in the United States of America

CPSIA compliance information: Batch #CS19GS. For further information contact Gareth Stevens, New York, New York at 1-800-542-2595.

Contents

A beautiful, **deserted** island where you can relax and get away from it all is many people's ideal vacation. But, what if the island was home to ghosts? Surrounded by water, you'd be trapped there until the next boat or plane out. It might be an idea to check out these spooky islands around the world before booking a dream vacation!

Sunbathers on Raisins Clair Beach, Guadaloupe, sometimes get a nasty surprise. Human teeth, bones, and coffin nails may appear in the sand right next to them! **Archaeologists** believe **erosion** by the waves is gradually exposing an old slave cemetery. An iron collar was found around the neck of one unearthed skeleton.

In 1862, a settler named John Morton rowed to a deserted island in Vancouver Harbor, Canada. He discovered hundreds of strange red cedar boxes up in the trees. The ancient boxes crumbled when he touched them, covering him with human bones! He had stumbled across an old **Squamish** tree-burial ground. Now known as Deadman's Island, loud clanging noises have been heard, along with the sound of footsteps and a woman sobbing.

DEADMAN'S ISLAND, AROUND 1910

Even if you don't believe in ghosts, being trapped on an island after dark can make your imagination run wild!

Isle of Wight, England

The Isle of Wight lies just off England's south coast. With haunted hotels, forts, castles, inns, houses, police stations, shops, and even offices, it is the most haunted island in Britain. It is hard to find a building on the island that isn't said to be haunted! Many people believe this is due to **ley lines** that pass through the island. Ley lines are imaginary lines between sacred places such as burial mounds or stone circles. Some people believe these lines contain **supernatural** energy, making it easy for spirits to appear there.

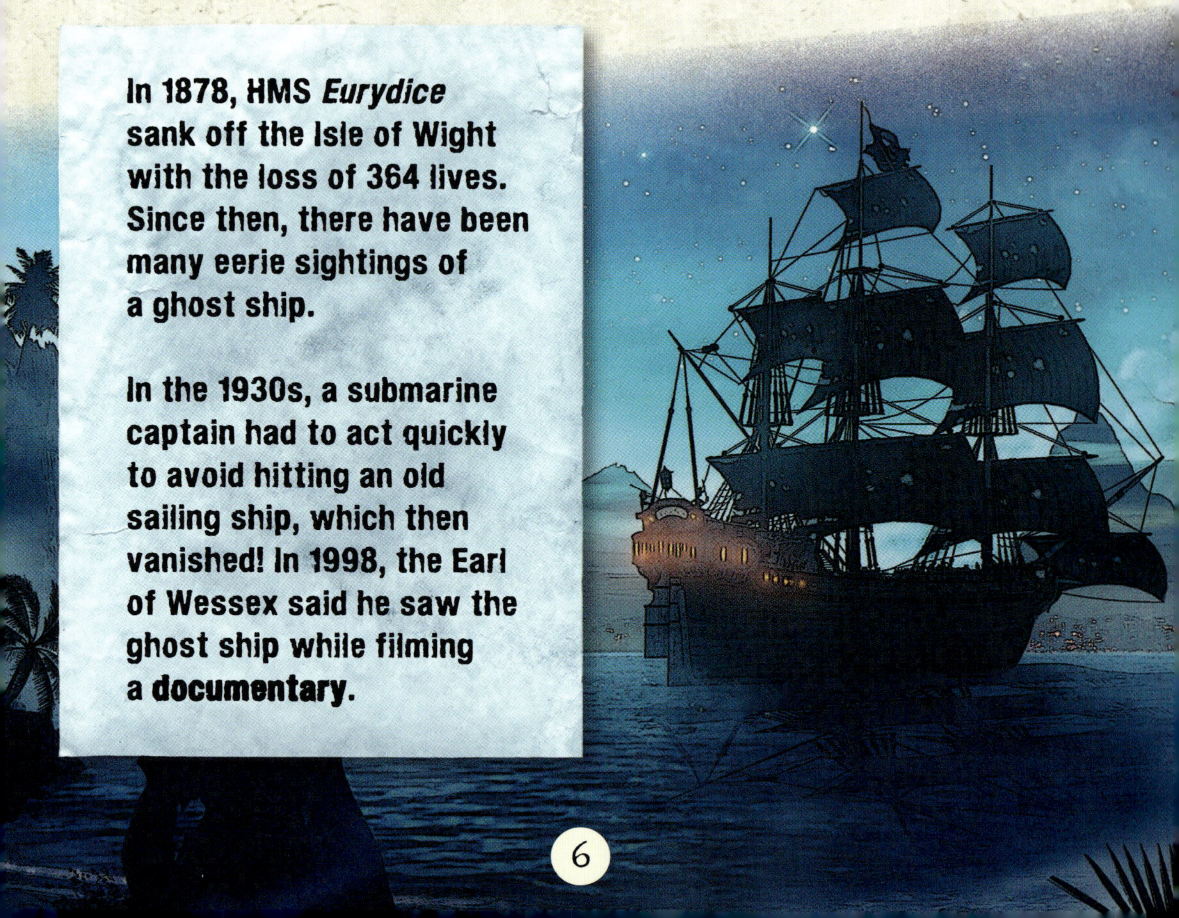

In 1878, HMS *Eurydice* sank off the Isle of Wight with the loss of 364 lives. Since then, there have been many eerie sightings of a ghost ship.

In the 1930s, a submarine captain had to act quickly to avoid hitting an old sailing ship, which then vanished! In 1998, the Earl of Wessex said he saw the ghost ship while filming a documentary.

The beautiful Botanical Gardens at Ventnor are haunted by the ghosts of patients from an old hospital that once stood on the site. In 1985, the **curator** of the gardens had an actual conversation with a ghost! The pale, thin man was wearing an old-fashioned suit, and said he was a hospital patient.

Knighton Gorges Manor was demolished in 1821, but sometimes on New Year's Eve the ghostly house reappears. Strange stone creatures are also said to appear on top of the remaining gateposts!

Island of the Dolls, Mexico

This deserted island in Lake Teshuilo, Mexico, is covered in creepy-looking dolls! Dolls hang from practically every tree and fence post. Why? In the 1920s, three young girls were playing near the water when one fell in and drowned. Since then, the island is believed to be haunted, and locals won't go there at night. In the 1950s, a man named Julian Santana Barrera left his family and went to live alone on the island. He believed the child's ghost started to speak to him, and he began to leave old dolls around the island for the girl to play with.

Local people believe the dolls are filled with the spirit of a girl who drowned on the island. People say they have seen the dolls move and whisper!

Julian collected more and more dolls to protect himself from her unhappy spirit. He believed she wanted to **lure** him to her watery grave. One day, Julian's nephew visited and found his uncle dead, facedown in a canal in the same spot the girl had drowned!

Julian Santana Barrera's ghost is said to haunt the island, too.

Mont Saint-Michel, France

The ancient monastery and abbey on the granite island of Mont Saint-Michel look like a fairy-tale castle. You can walk to the island at **low tide**. At **high tide**, the sea rises quickly and cuts the island off from the mainland. Monks would risk the dangerous tides and sinking sands on pilgrimages to the island. Spooky phantom monks are sometimes seen wandering the island. Perhaps the men drowned on their journey?

There is said to be a secret tunnel from the island of Tombelaine to Mont Saint-Michel. In the 1600s, Tombelaine's owner, Nicolas Fouquet, got trapped there by the tide. He magically appeared at a house on Mont Saint-Michel!

The ghost of Louis d'Estouteville is said to haunt the island. In 1434, he was the commander of the garrison on the island. He defended the abbey against an English invasion. His men killed around 2,000 enemy soldiers in a bloody battle on the beach, said to have turned the sand red. The English retreated to their garrison on Tombelaine and never attacked the island again. Louis d'Estouteville later retook Tombelaine. His ghost still stands guard, ready to defend Mont Saint-Michel.

MONT SAINT-MICHEL

Nan Madol, Micronesia

Micronesia is made up of many tiny tropical islands. Nan Madol is one of the smallest, and home to a mysterious ancient city. Giant **basalt** columns, weighing as much as 50 tons each, were used to build the city, on top of a coral reef. Experts believe the city was a burial site and religious center. There is no record of when the city was built, but people have lived on Nan Madol for around 2,000 years.

Two giant brothers are said to have built Nan Madol using magical powers, helped by a flying dragon!

NAN MADOL

The city has many mysteries. Where did the huge rocks come from? How were they brought there? How did the people build the city without machinery? Perhaps Nan Madol really was built by magic and giants!

THE HUGE BASALT COLUMNS

Locals avoid Nan Madol. They believe it is cursed. Only a few brave ones will take tourists there, and only in daylight. Strange glowing **orbs** are seen hovering there after dark! In the early 1900s, despite being warned not to, a German island governor opened an ancient coffin. In it was a giant skeleton. That night there was a wild storm. The governor heard the sound of a conch shell blowing, and then saw floating balls of light. A few hours later, he was dead. Doctors could not find any reason why he died.

Seguin Island, Maine

Loneliness can drive you mad. In the mid-1800s, a lighthouse keeper and his wife lived on this rocky island off the coast of Maine. Seguin Island lighthouse protected sailors from hitting the dangerous rocks scattered around the coastline. Keeping the light burning was a lonely job. To cheer themselves up, they had a piano shipped to the island. The lighthouse keeper's wife chose a tune to play, and practiced it day and night.

SEGUIN LIGHTHOUSE

Over and over, the lighthouse keeper's wife played the same tune. She refused to play any other. Eventually the lighthouse keeper snapped, and attacked her piano with an ax! He then murdered her, and killed himself. When the lighthouse closed, one of the men clearing the house saw the keeper's ghost. The ghost warned them to leave his house alone. The boat carrying his furniture mysteriously sank the next day.

Visitors to the island have heard the sound of piano music coming from the lighthouse! Others have seen the lighthouse keeper walking the island, holding his ax.

Ross Island, India

This small island in South Andaman, India, was once a British settlement. The British first used the island as a prison, housing Indians who refused to obey their laws. They built grand houses, dance halls, and swimming pools. Now, Ross Island is deserted.

AN ABANDONED COLONIAL BUILDING

The jungle is gradually taking back Ross Island's abandoned buildings. The grand houses now have spooky trees growing out of them!

The island was covered in dense jungle when the British first arrived with 200 convicts. The prisoners were forced to clear the land while the officers stayed in their ships. It was dangerous work. The jungle was so dense that if a tree was cut it had nowhere to fall. The water was not safe to drink and most of the prisoners became ill and died. Life was brutal. Two months after the colony was established, the British hung 81 convicts who had tried to escape.

Over 3,000 prisoners died on Ross Island. It is not surprising the island seems spooky! The graves near this abandoned church would have been for British dead. Prisoners were buried in the sand, with no coffin or ceremony.

THE RUINS OF THE PROTESTANT CHURCH

North Brother Island, New York

In the middle of the East River, in busy New York City, lies North Brother Island. In 1885, a quarantine hospital was built on the uninhabited island. Riverside Hospital cared for people suffering from **contagious** diseases such as typhoid, smallpox, and yellow fever. Now abandoned, it is creepily quiet. The surrounding empty forest muffles the sound of the bustling city life across the water.

North Brother Island is now closed to the public, and is a bird sanctuary. The spooky old hospital buildings lie deserted.

THE OLD HOSPITAL

"TYPHOID MARY" (LEFT) AT RIVERSIDE HOSPITAL

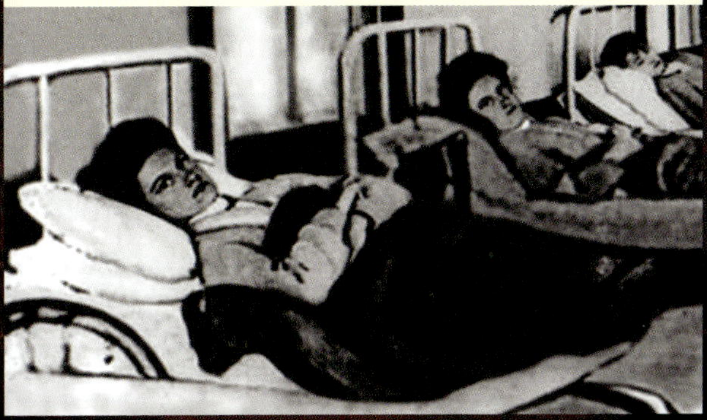

"Typhoid Mary" was the hospital's most famous patient. She is thought to have given over 50 people typhoid fever, killing three of them. Although she was never ill from the disease herself, she was forced to stay at the hospital for nearly 30 years!

A ghostly woman has been seen in the old hospital corridors. Could it be Typhoid Mary? Or perhaps it is one of over 1,000 people who drowned in a steamship accident nearby.

In 1904, the *General Slocum* caught fire and sank. Packed full of people on a church picnic outing, their waterlogged clothes weighed them down in the water. Hospital staff helped pull 321 survivors from the river. Since then, weeping ghosts are said to wander the island.

VICTIMS BEING BROUGHT ASHORE

Norfolk Island, Australia

This remote island was used by the British as a prison. Prisoners named the island "Hell on Earth" because of the tough conditions and cruel punishments. Convicts were kept in chains with little food and forced to do hard labor. It seems some of the prisoners may have stuck around to get revenge!

Around half the people now living on the island say they have seen a ghost there. The sound of clanging chains is heard around the island. A ghostly uniformed soldier and a well-dressed lady have been seen walking along the road by the officers' houses, known as Quality Row.

THE CEMETERY GRAVESTONES TELL OF MURDERS, EXECUTIONS, AND DROWNINGS

A stream on the island sometimes flooded, so chain gangs of prisoners were made to build a bridge. During the building, one of the work gangs is said to have murdered a guard and walled his body up in the bridge! The next day, the guard's replacement saw blood oozing from the wall. Now known as the Bloody Bridge, it is still stained a strange red color.

THE BLOODY BRIDGE

The Convict Store is one of the most haunted sites. A ghost is often seen walking down the stairs. People believe he may be a convict who drowned on the island, or a soldier.

Daksa Island, Croatia

The beautiful city of Dubrovnik lies on the Croatian coast. The historic city attracts thousands of visitors. But just off the mainland, the island of Daksa lies empty and unvisited. Why? The island is supposedly haunted!

Near the end of World War II, people thought to have sided with the **Nazis** were rounded up and rowed out to the island of Daksa. There, they were shot by firing squad. Their families were warned not to search for their loved ones. Their bodies lay on the island in two mass graves for 60 years! Their ghosts are said to haunt the island.

Daksa was up for sale recently, but no one wanted to buy it. Archaeologists aren't sure they have found all of the murdered men's bodies yet!

Dubrovnik Harbor bustles with day-trippers' boats heading to islands along the coast. But local ferrymen won't go to Daksa, or its neighbor, Lokrum. Monks forced to leave Lokrum cursed the island, and bad luck is believed to fall on anyone who visits there now.

Okinawa Island, Japan

In the last months of World War II, Okinawa was invaded by U.S. troops. During the 82-day battle, 12,500 American and 95,000 Japanese soldiers were killed. Around 100,000 ordinary Japanese people also died in the fighting. With this many violent deaths, it is not surprising Okinawa is believed to be haunted.

Not all the Japanese were killed by American hands. Many killed themselves to avoid the dishonor of being captured or fear of being tortured. The cliffs at Itoman were the site of fierce fighting. Many soldiers chose to jump to their deaths.

GHOST JUMPERS AND SPOOKY FACES IN THE WAVES HAVE BEEN SEEN HERE!

Over 2,000 Japanese sailors died defending Okinawa's underground headquarters. The tunnels are now haunted. People have reported feeling a force grabbing their legs, trying to keep them from leaving.

On Okinawa, there is a small park with a tall, white memorial built on it. It was built to help ward off evil spirits that haunted the spot! According to legend, the first owner of the land died, and passed it to a friend in their will. After a few days, the friend also died. Shortly afterwards, the next owner of the land died. This kept happening until the government stepped in, bought the land, and built the memorial!

Holy Island, England

You can drive to Holy Island when the tide is out. But keep your eye on the clock! At high tide, the island is completely cut off from the mainland. An ancient priory on Holy Island houses the burial place of Saint Cuthbert and became a place of **pilgrimage**. **Viking** raids and local robbers forced the monks to leave the island, taking the body of Saint Cuthbert with them.

Saint Cuthbert is said to haunt the island still, and can often be seen at high tide on nights with a full moon.

It may seem spooky that the monks dug up the dead saint after all those years. What is even spookier is that when they did, instead of finding bones, his body is said to have been in perfect condition!

THE PRIORY

Lindisfarne Castle is perched on top of a rocky hill on the island. Several visitors have seen a ghostly white dog there. It jumps out at passersby and then slinks back into the ruins where it came from.

Alcatraz Island, California

In the cold, choppy waters of San Francisco Bay lies the prison island of Alcatraz. The harsh prison was home to many **notorious** prisoners, such as gangster Al Capone and George "Machine Gun" Kelly. The prison is said to be haunted by several of its old inmates. Sobbing and moaning have been heard from the cells. People have also reported smelling smoke, or suddenly feeling ice cold!

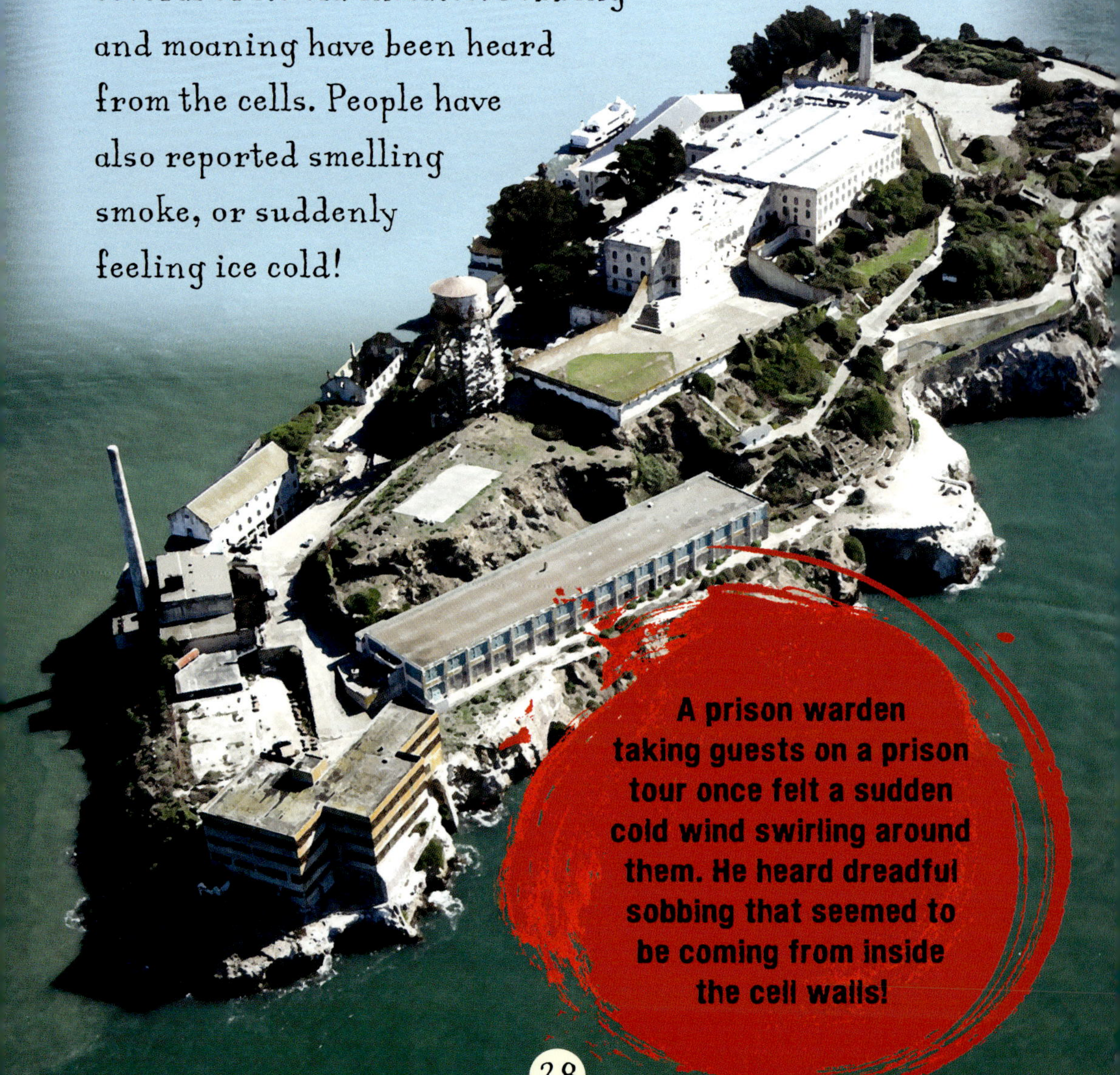

A prison warden taking guests on a prison tour once felt a sudden cold wind swirling around them. He heard dreadful sobbing that seemed to be coming from inside the cell walls!

Unruly prisoners were put in "The Hole." Hole cell 14D is always colder than the other cells. One prisoner locked in 14D screamed all night to be let out, saying he could see a creature with glowing eyes. The next morning he was found strangled. Was he murdered by a ghost, or by a guard, sick of his screams?

When guards did a head count the next day, there were too many men. There for a moment, at the end of the line, was the face of the dead man!

A park ranger heard the haunting sound of a banjo coming from the prison showers. Famous inmate Al Capone liked to play the banjo. He did not like going out to the prison yard, as he feared for his life. He got permission to practice playing his banjo in the shower room. Was the banjo music played by the ghost of gangster Al Capone?

Glossary

archaeologists people who study past human life by examining old buildings and tools

basalt a dark gray to black igneous rock

contagious likely to be passed on via contact

curator a person in charge of a museum

deserted abandoned

documentary a program presenting actual events or facts about something

erosion being worn away

high tide the tide when the water is at its greatest height

ley line an imaginary line between important places believed to be the site of an old path

low tide the tide when the water is at its lowest height

lure to tempt or lead away

Nazis the German fascist party controlling Germany from 1933 to 1945

notorious widely and unfavorably known

orbs objects in the shape of a ball

pilgrimage a journey of a pilgrim

Squamish a member of an American Indian people of British Columbia

supernatural attributed to a ghost or spirit

Viking Scandinavians who raided Europe in the 8th to 10th centuries

Further Reading

Chandler, Matt. *Alcatraz: A Chilling Interactive Adventure (You Choose: Haunted Places)*. Mankato, MN: Capstone Press, 2016.

Williams, Dinah. *Creepy Islands (Scary Places)*. New York, NY: Bearport Publishing, 2014.

Website

KidzSearch encyclopedia pages about Norfolk Island and Alcatraz
https://wiki.kidzsearch.com/wiki/Norfolk_Island
https://wiki.kidzsearch.com/wiki/Alcatraz_Island

Publisher's note to educators and parents: Our editors have carefully reviewed these websites to ensure that they are suitable for students. Many websites change frequently, however, and we cannot guarantee that a site's future contents will continue to meet our high standards of quality and educational value. Be advised that students should be closely supervised whenever they access the Internet.

Index

Don't be scared! Most people don't believe ghosts are real at all. No one has ever scientifically proven they exist. But it can be fun to get yourself a little spooked!